Divisor Drips and Square Root Waves

Prime Numbers are the Holes in
Complex Composite Number Patterns

© 2010 Jeffrey Ventrella

Ventrella, Jeffrey, J.

Divisor Drips and Square Root Waves – Prime Numbers are the Holes in Complex Composite Number Patterns

Book web site: www.divisorplot.com

Eyebrain Books (www.eyebrainbooks.com)

ISBN 978-0-9830546-1-0

Distributed by Lulu.com

Cover design by Jeffrey Ventrella

Second Edition

Contents

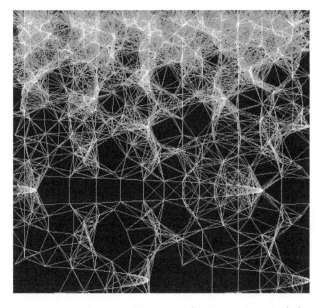

Connecting nearby pairs of divisors in the divisor plot in both the x and y dimensions, with brighter lines indicating closer divisors.

A Note to the Reader

This book is intended for people of all ages and all levels of mathematical expertise. All I ask is that you have at least one eye, a brain, and that you know how to count. It also helps if you have a passion for patterns, and that you know some basic symbols (like the square root symbol: $\sqrt{}$, or the symbol for a factorial number: !). Having some basic familiarity with prime numbers, composite numbers, and basic number theory also helps. I have kept the math notation to a minimum – but that's appropriate...since I am not a mathematician! I am a visual language professional who has stumbled upon a set of mathematical concepts through my explorations in geometry, and a deep lifelong love of patterns.

This book does not put forth theorems or proofs – an important part of the mathematical process. But it does put forth many hypotheses – all based on the creation of pictures and graphs. In fact it is very rich in terms of another, very important, part of mathematics, which is universal and primal: pattern finding. This book will stimulate your mind by showing spatial relationships and new connections. It points the way towards seeing things in a way that may have been clouded in the past by old paradigms. It also takes advantage of the power of computer graphics data visualization, which is not a part of classical mathematics. Seeing patterns (or hearing patterns, or feeling patterns) is the fundamental basis of math. That is the philosophical foundation of this book.

Even if you simply open this book and gaze at the pictures in a semi-conscious trance, I would be happy. Your visual mind will be doing its own special kind of mathematics. And it may not surface to your conscious mind for another twenty years. That's fine with me: I'm in no rush.

1. A Pattern-Finding Journey

Write the numbers one through ten.

1 2 3 4 5 6 7 8 9 10

1	2	3	4	5	6	7	8	9	10
1	1	1	1	1	1	1	1	1	1
	2		2		2		2		2
		3			3			3	
			4				4		
				5					5
					6				
						7			
							8		
								9	
									10

Four of those numbers are prime: 2, 3, 5, and 7. They have no integer divisors other than 1 and themselves. Now, write the integer divisors of these ten numbers in columns underneath, spaced out vertically according to their sizes, as shown here. As you would expect, there are visual gaps below the primes.

The other numbers have more divisors than 2. They partially fill the right-triangular area below the row of 1's, and above the diagonal string of numbers at the bottom-left. These are the *composite* numbers. And if you ask me, they are much more interesting than the primes!

You may not think this is a very interesting pattern. But what if you keep extending the number line out really far, to a big number, like, say, *nine quintillion*? Out there, you will witness some amazing stuff. That stuff is what this book is about.

Once, when I was a young boy, I got a sheet of paper and a pencil, and started plotting this graph, just for fun. After plotting out the numbers up to a hundred, I began to see patterns. At the time, I had never heard of the *Sieve of Eratosthenes*, but that is essentially what I

was visualizing. Little did I know that twenty years later I would gaze at the same graph of numbers – only this time on a computer screen.

According to the mathematician Gregory Chaitin, "A concept is only as good as the theorems that it leads to!...instead of primes, perhaps we should be concerned with the opposite, with the maximally divisible numbers!" [1]. I read this statement in Chaitin's book *MetaMath!*, several decades after making that pencil drawing. It got me remembering those patterns and the curiosity it provoked. Having only gotten as far as the introduction of the book, I dropped it and ran to my computer. It may have been Chaitin's excessive use of exclamation marks that got me charged up, but I suspect it was something more!!!

I decided to return to this drawing and explore it in more depth. So I created an interactive computer visualization (which is now available at www.divisorplot.com). It allows exploration of large numbers, with a greater range of divisors. As I worked on the interactive tools to explore this space of numbers, I found ever more patterns. I want to share with you some of the excitement of these discoveries.

Let's scan a little farther out on the number line now. In the graph below, notice the patterns that start to emerge in the upper-right area.

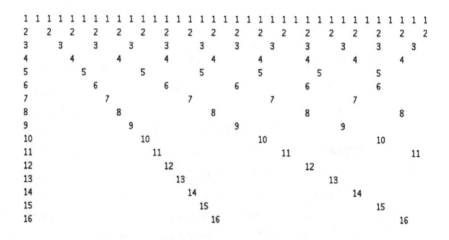

If we zoom the view out even further and change the numerals to dots, we see even more patterns. Here are the divisors ranging from 1 to 120 for a section of the number line in the vicinity of 151,080.

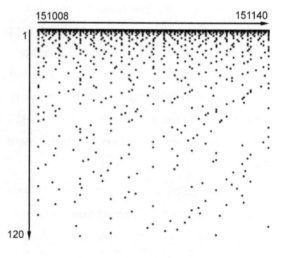

Why do these patterns appear complex, almost random? Especially considering the simplicity of the rule that is used to plot them. They exhibit apparent randomness, yes – but also some order. Fodder for the pattern-hungry human brain. That is really what this book is about – a quest to understand why these patterns exist.

This quest is explained from the standpoint of a non-mathematician: a visual language professional who, in the process of seeking out these patterns, *becomes* a mathematician, in the most universal and general sense – in the sense that all humans are mathematicians. It's just that most people speak a mathematical language of pictures, physical structures, gestures, music, and the rhythms of speech, rather than using a specialized alphabet of symbols connected together to make math notation.

While the creation of theorems and proofs may be the defining pinnacle of mathematics, the explorations that lead to them is universal to all humans. This very human kind of pattern-finding is what many educators believe we should encourage young students to experience: to internalize the beauty and value of mathematics, before having to read dense text books full of dry equations and disembodied formulas, devoid of purpose and stripped of aesthetics. Young or old, professional or novice, we are all pattern-finders.

Pattern-finding is the very creative, very human side of mathematics. In *The Music of the Primes*, Marcus du Sautoy explains how mathematicians often fluctuate between feeling that they are being creative and a sense that they are uncovering absolute truths. He says:

"Although the primes, and other aspects of mathematics, transcend cultural barriers, much of mathematics is creative and a product of the human psyche. Proofs, the stories mathematicians tell about their subject, can often be narrated in different ways. It is likely that Wiles's proof of Fermat's Last Theorem would be as mysterious to aliens as listening to Wagner's Ring cycle. Mathematics is a creative act under constraints – like writing poetry or playing the blues. Mathematicians are bound by the logical steps they must take in crafting their proofs. Yet within such constraints there is still a lot of freedom. Indeed, the beauty of creating under constraints is that you get pushed in new directions and find things you might never have expected to discover unaided. The primes are like notes in a scale, and each culture has chosen to play these notes in its own particular way, revealing more about historical and social influences than one might expect. The story of the primes is a social mirror as much as the discovery of timeless truths" [3].

Seeing things from different perspectives is what du Sautoy is talking about. But while he suggests that the prime numbers are "notes in a scale", and that each culture plays these notes in a different way, I believe that the primes are not like notes at all. They are the *silent spaces between notes*. The notes comprise a magnificent symphony, full of beautiful symmetry. And the instruments used to play that symphony are the *composite numbers*.

An important paradigm shift that this book follows is the idea that prime numbers are not the stars of the show. They are not the building blocks of all numbers. The stars of the show are the composite numbers, with symmetry and beautiful fractal-like structure that grows as you venture out along the number line to larger and larger numbers.

I hope that this book will make you think of "number" in a different way than it is typically described: not as a dry, boring symbol on a piece of paper, or as a concept that expresses a single quantity, but as a pattern situated inside a society of overlapping patterns with deep complex structure. If you listen closely to an extremely large composite number, you can hear a symphony playing inside. And that's not all: *every number* has it's own unique symphonic composition. And the primes? They don't make any sound.

Integer, Pattern, and Human Intelligence

While gazing at these divisor dots, rendered in white on a black background (as I prefer to render them on the computer screen), I have the sensation of being an ancient astronomer trying to find some order in the chaos. In the illustration below of a starry sky at dusk, it looks as if the stars are scattered randomly, but they are actually plotted out according to this very simple rule.

As you gaze at this *Sky of Divisors*, you may find Chariots, Big Bears, and Scorpions, as the ancient astronomers did. But for me, the most interesting patterns are the ones that reveal mathematical truths. Karl Sabbagh believes that if there is intelligent life elsewhere in the universe, it will be capable of numerical counting. "The stars in the sky are discrete points and cry out to be counted by intelligent beings throughout the universe (at least the ones who can see)." [8].

Counting naturally leads to truths such as 2+2=4, as well as all integer math, primes. etc. Leopold Kronecker said, "God created the integers; the rest is man's doing." We have magnificent occipital lobes, and our brains are wired to find patterns, at all levels - consciously and unconsciously. My exploration of these patterns begins with my visual pattern-seeking brain, and progressively applies language and math to my discoveries. I believe this is the natural trajectory of human mathematics.

Thinking Big

Rudy Rucker says, "There are infinitely many natural numbers. They surround us in all dimensions like an ocean without shores. Compared to the ocean of number, our whole starry sky, all that is, is less than a germ in the gut of a tube worm warming itself by a volcanic vent at the bottom of the ten-kilometer-deep Marina Trench" [7]. Rucker uses colorful language to make a point: we are not able to grasp the vastness of really large numbers (such as ten to the power of one million).

But we *can* grasp patterns very well.

Small numbers are experienced quite easily, especially the very small numbers less than about 5, which are the subitizable ones (most of us can grasp them instantly in our minds without having to count: think of walking into a kitchen and noticing three apples in a bowl on the table). But as numbers get bigger, we need patterning, counting, iteration, to apprehend them. That's why we use the base ten (or any base) to clumpify numbers into scaling chunks. When numbers are *really* big, they can only be experienced as *patterns*.

As far as the brain is concerned, it may be that *all* numbers are processed as patterns (even the subitizable ones, except that our brains have special efficient neural networks that create what feels like instant recognition). Recent brain research has identified distinct patterns in the human parietal cortex associated with numerical processing for small numbers, and so we may soon find out more about this neural patterning.

The brilliant mathematician Ramanujan may have had abnormal neural networks allowing him to experience large primes with the same immediacy and instant clarity as a child apprehending three apples. Experiencing numbers really just comes down to patterns on the subconscious level (like everything else). But what really matters for communicating numbers are the languages we use to name them and the visualizations we use to understand them.

The larger the number, the harder it is for the human brain to grok it as a single quantity. And in fact, given the spectacular symmetry and interwoven internal structure found in the number 20! (twenty factorial), it is not very useful to think of it as a single quantity: 2,432,902,008,176,640,000. There is much more going on inside that number.

Overlapping Patterns

Based on the theories of Maxwell, Einstein, Schroedinger, de Broglie, Clifford, Wheeler, Feynman, and many others, one might conclude that everything in the universe can be described in terms of overlapping waves. Ray Tomes [12] suggests that the universe consists of many standing waves of many frequencies and overlapping in many ways. The combination of these waves produce harmonics.

Thomasson [11], Wolfram [14], and others, have generated small variations of the graph I discovered to illustrate the distribution of primes. A few of these are shown here.

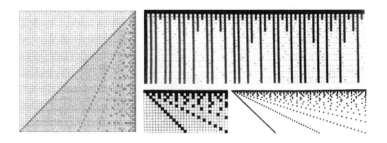

I presented my discoveries in October of 2007 at the International Conference on Complex Systems in Boston [13]. Since publishing the web site on divisorplot.com, many fellow prime number pattern explorers have contacted me, and some of their findings are shared in this book.

David Cox published similar findings in 2008, in a paper called *Visualizing the Sieve of Eratosthenes* [2]. An image reproduced from Cox's paper is shown below. We will address a few of Cox's observations later on.

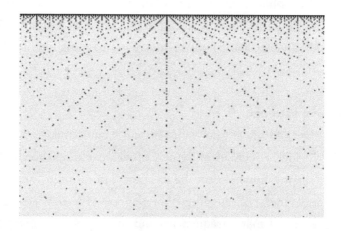

Building Blocks or Empty Spaces?

We hear of primes described as the "building blocks" of all numbers. Let's turn that concept on its head. Instead, let's think of primes as the negative spaces behind overlapping objects.

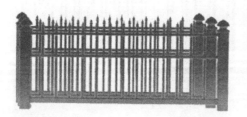 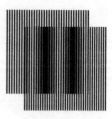

Imagine a series of picket fences stacked in front of each other. Each picket fence has different spacing between its wooden slats. The superimposition of fences creates line moiré patterns.

Consider the Sieve of Eratosthenes, a process where each stage involves hopping along the number line with increasingly larger steps. This activity progressively stamps out the composite numbers, to identify primes. It's kind of like stacking these picket fences, each one with a larger gap between its slats - to eliminate the holes. Some holes will always remain. Those are the primes.

Asking the Wrong Questions

People are still asking, "What is the formula for the distribution of the primes on the number line?" "How can we predict when the next prime number will occur?" "What is the *heartbeat* of the primes?"

The heartbeat, by all accounts, has been fibrillating since the beginning of time, and its erratic behavior shows no sign of stopping. The problem is that these questions are based on a mental model that is stuck with marching along the number line from 0 to infinity. It is hyperlinear. The distribution of prime numbers might be better understood as the artifact of overlapping composite number patterns. For instance, take a look at the diagram on the next page of the first 100 primes against the graph of divisors.

I selected the composite numbers 42 and 60 as examples of how their immediate prime neighbors exhibit left-right symmetry. Actually, I have been told by a mathematician friend of mine that this symmetry is not just in the immediate neighborhood, but that it extends well beyond. And the reason that this symmetry appears to break down after a certain distance is because of the overlapping effect of many composite number patterns – each one having its own symmetrical pattern. Later on in the book we will explore more forms of symmetry about certain composite numbers.

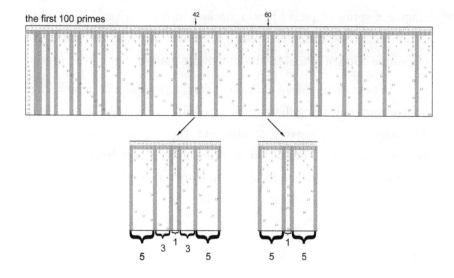

the first 100 primes

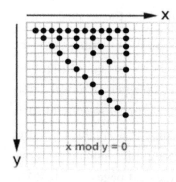

x mod y = 0

A Definition

The graph I discovered when I was young doesn't appear to have a name, even though small versions of it have appeared at various times in the literature. I call this graph the "divisor plot". It can be defined as the set of all integer locations in the x,y plane (where y is positive) for which x mod y = 0. Let us call these integer locations "divisors". As integer locations, these divisors lie on a 2D lattice with cells of size 1. The y coordinate of each location is a divisor of x. I prefer to make the y axis point downward, so that higher y values are lower. It could just as easily be plotted the opposite way, but I find this way to be easiest for visualization.

Unfurling the Divisor Function

The number of divisors of an integer x (called the *divisor function*) is denoted as d(x). In this book, I will refer to the *actual set* of the divisors of x as Dx. As an example, D6 = {1, 2, 3, 6}. Every Dx is unique – and that fact is related to the fundamental theorem of arithmetic, which states that every integer can be described as a unique product of prime numbers: no two integers have the same set of prime number divisors. Similarly, no two integers have the same Dx.

The *divisor function* is a counting of the number of divisors for an integer. If you plot a graph of the divisor function across the number line, you will notice that it is quite jaggy. This is directly related to the famously jaggy distribution of primes – the fibrillating heartbeat. Imagine compressing the divisor plot so that all the divisors get stacked up into vertical columns. The divisor function graph can be thought of as this vertical stacking of divisors in the divisor plot.

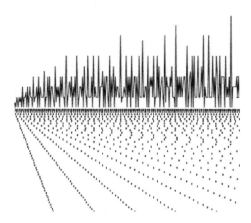

Sometimes, the way to understand something that is seemingly random is to see it as *ground* instead of *figure*, or as the shadow of something in a higher dimension. Perhaps that is how we should think of the prime numbers.

Numbers are typically considered as lying on a one-dimensional line. Think instead of the prime numbers as shadows cast by something in a higher dimension. Perhaps this is why Bernhard Riemann was able to discover a new way to look at the primes: he deployed the complex plane, a rich two-dimensional context within which to discover something about the distribution of primes [6].

Let's follow Chaitin's call to study the maximally-composite numbers instead of the primes. Composites are the generators of all pattern. Prime numbers are the holes, the shadows, the *ground* behind the *figure*. What passes through the Sieve of Eratosthenes is far less interesting than the Sieve itself. Likewise, the tools we use to generate random sequences such as the Golden Ratio and Pi (tools like the Fibonacci sequence and Buffon's Needle) are much more interesting than the random sequences themselves. After all, there is no information in random sequences. Why bother spending so much time looking at them?

2. Divisor Drips and Reflection Rays

In the divisor plot, relatively dense strings of divisors can be seen beneath some numbers, like dripping water. I call these "divisor drips". That's just a poetic name for numbers that have lots of divisors (Dx), such as the *highly composite numbers* (numbers that have more divisors than any lesser number).

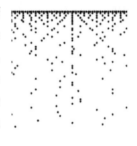

On either side of dense divisor drips you can often detect radiating lines projecting outward and downward. I call these "reflection rays". These are reflections of the divisor drip, equivalent to addition or subtraction of multiples of y to the y coordinates of divisors. Reflection rays are a natural outcome of dense divisor drips. You could also think of the reflection rays associated with a particular divisor drip Dx as the set of common multiples that x shares with other numbers.

The illustration below shows D0, and the first 4 of its positive reflection rays, indicated with arrows. Also shown are a few of the reflection rays (y<5) of D12, indicated with thin lines. Notice that there is another clearly-visible divisor drip, similar to the one at D12, a bit farther to the right. Just take a guess at what that number is without counting up to that location. If you guessed that it is 24, you would be correct! With this small range of the number line, it is not hard to guess the numbers simply by looking at the divisor drips (or the absence of them).

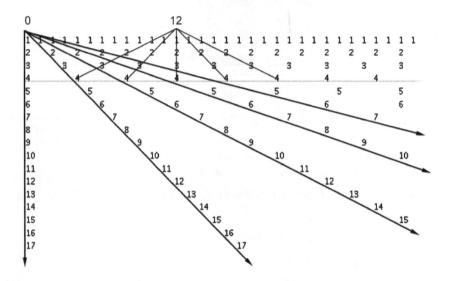

In D24, you may have noticed the divisor 8 in the drip, which you may have used as your clue. You might have also noticed the '5' sticking out just to the right of the D24 drip. It is a lonely divisor: the square root of 25. Finally, you can probably easily guess what the last two numbers in this graph are without actually counting up to them.

A kind of portraiture of numbers is revealed as we study this picture. If you study it long enough, you might start to detect certain social trends, such as the way twin primes often snuggle up to either side of strong composite numbers.

The image below shows x at 12! (or *12 factorial*, which is equal to 1 x 2 x 3 x 4 x 5 x 6x 7 x 8 x 9 x 10 x 11 x 12, or 479,001,600). It has a strong divisor drip and clearly-visible reflection rays.

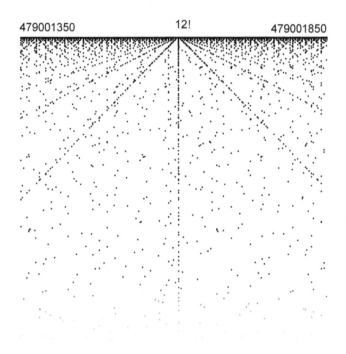

Definition of "Zero Reflection Ray"

Since every integer could be considered as a divisor of 0 (when multiplied by 0), 0 is considered here as the ultimate highly composite number – having a completely solid divisor drip, and subsequent reflection rays. There are infinitely many zero reflection rays Z numbered n from 1 to infinity. Zero reflection ray Zn is defined as the ray originating at (0,0), and having slope 1/-n. Each Zn has an ordinal set of divisors lying on it. The higher the value of n, the more sparse the divisors along the ray. Every divisor in the divisor plot is a member of one Zn, and *only one*.

Why is Zero like Twelve Factorial?

If we allow the divisor plot to include negative x, we get the pattern shown below at left. We know that 12! has 1 through 12 as divisors. (It has many other divisors as well). The right half of the image shows that the divisor pattern at 12! is identical to the pattern at 0 for all y less than 13.

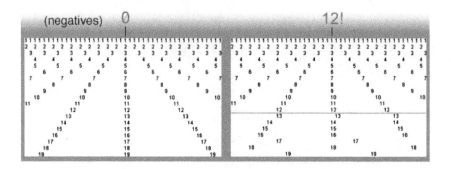

In the divisor plot, any x = n! will look like the zero region among the first n divisors. Let's think bigger now, and consider the number 25! For the first 25 divisors, the region in the divisor plot near this number looks identical to the region near zero.

The bigger the factorial number, the more its neighborhood looks like the neighborhood of 0. I suspect that not only the immediate region of the n! but the entire pattern looks identical to 0, because it is a repeating pattern, a pattern that repeats itself every n! numbers. To explore this idea, below are some examples of patterns of 3!, 4!, and 5! In each case, the solid divisor drip of length n repeats itself every n! number. However, there may be other repetitions of n-length divisor drips. For instance, notice the repetition of a length-4 divisor drip at 12, which occurs before 4! In the illustration below. Also, not shown here is a repetition of a 5-length divisor drip at 60, which occurs before 5!

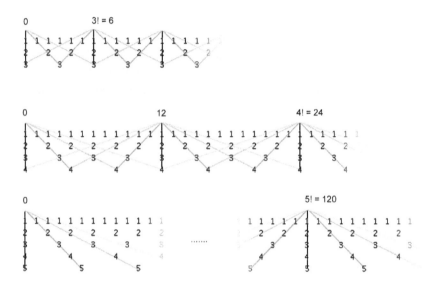

Structure

A number like 25! Is not very interesting when viewed as a one-dimensional string of digits (as shown here in base 10):

$$15,511,210,043,330,985,984,000,000$$

But there is hidden structure in this number, as revealed in the divisor plot (and possibly other visual representations). Compare this to the cells in a grasshopper. If you could line the millions of grasshopper cells in a row, it would be a long row indeed. Impressive in sheer length, but not very impressive otherwise. Only when the cells are arranged in the form of a  grasshopper can we appreciate the beauty and function of this insect. Most importantly, a single string of cells is not capable of jumping over a mushroom.

Primeless Number Segments

One way to find an arbitrarily long contiguous series of composite numbers on the number line is to choose a factorial n! The numbers n!+2, n!+3, n!+4...n!+n comprise a contiguous sequence with no primes. The illustration below shows 7! with such a sequence highlighted. The sequence is in fact longer than 7, as indicated here by the divisors 8, 9 and 10 in the first positive reflection ray.

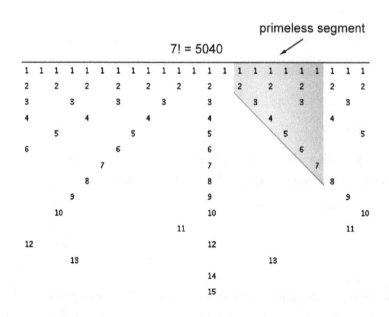

primeless segment

7! = 5040

Portrait of a Factorial

What is now coming into focus is a two-dimensional portrait of a factorial number, or more accurately: the number plus its immediate 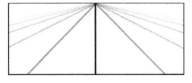 neighborhood. As viewed in the divisor plot, the divisor drip of a factorial n! has no gaps among the first n divisors. But there is another interesting feature of this factorial portrait. The associated reflection rays (specifically the first set on either side) each represent a contiguous set of composite numbers. In the example of 7! we could just as easily apply the same principle to the numbers to the left-side of the divisor drip: those numbers are also composite.

The two numbers immediately to the left and to the right of n! are special, however. They *may* or *may not* be composite numbers.

Patterns in Time

The illustration on the next page shows an imaginary scene with 6 objects with regularly-blinking lights. They start lined-up at the left of a track, move to the right at a constant speed, and then stop at the right side. If object 1 blinked once every second, object 2 blinked once every 2 seconds, object 3 once every 3 seconds, and so-on, and if they all started blinking at the same time at the start, then the resulting timed-exposure photograph would be an exact replica of the divisor plot pattern.

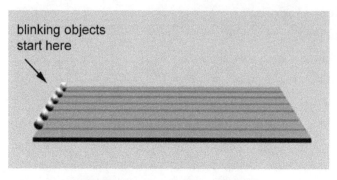

blinking objects
start here

...and move to here

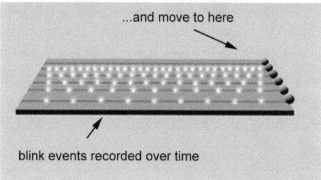

blink events recorded over time

Musical Polyrhythms

It is easy to compare the first 3 or 4 rows in the divisor plot to musical polyrhythm. For instance, a jazz, rock, or traditional African rhythm might juxtapose periods of 2 and 3, combined in various ways to create composite periods of 6, 12, etc. Periods of 2 and 3 (and their multiples) come naturally to the ear (and to dancing feet). We rarely encounter 5, 7, or other prime number periods in popular music. However, classical Western, African, and Indian music sometimes incorporates small prime number beats such as 5 or 7, juxtaposed against 4 or 8.

Here is a diagram showing a 2 against 3 polyrhythm.

Notice that each down-beat (when both rhythms have an X in the box) creates a miniature divisor drip, and that on either side are empty spaces - analogous to twin primes on the number line.

.

Rows

As we have just seen, it is useful to classify divisors in ways besides being members of a vertical divisor drip (Dx), or as members of an angled zero reflection ray (Zn). We can also classify them as existing in rows (seen as periodic signals moving from left to right). This is one way to visualize the Sieve of Eratosthenes. Let's refer to the horizontal rows that contain divisors as R. It is equivalent to the integer values of y. Later, we will see that there are even more ways to classify divisors, and they are much more interesting, visually and mathematically.

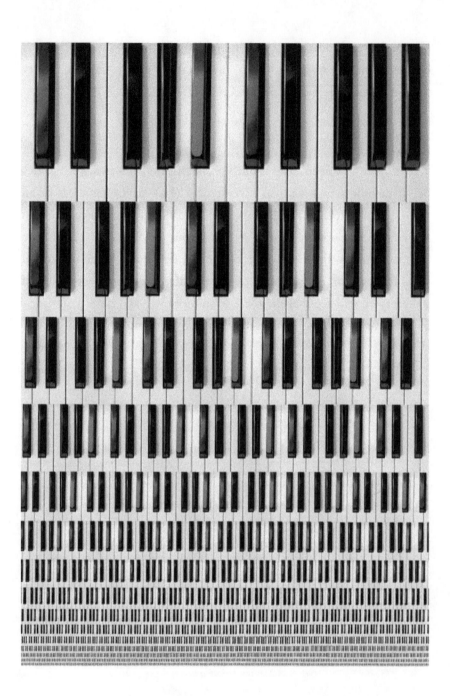

3. The Square Root Spine

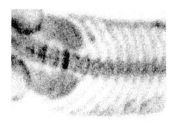

A curved spine arches through the divisor plot: the *square root boundary*. It defines an axis of symmetry. The divisor plot is fundamentally two-dimensional, and this is because multiplication is a tango for two: all divisors come in pairs, and those pairs lie on either side of the spine. This fact is fundamental to much of the patterning in the divisor plot. The illustration below shows the beginning of the curve.

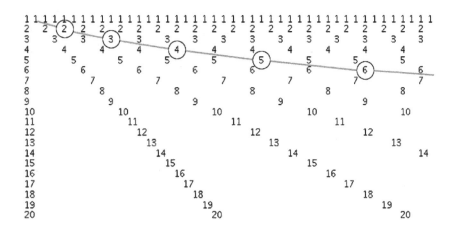

In this image, the square roots of the first six perfect squares, (1, 4, 9, 16, 25, 36) are highlighted with circles. This boundary becomes increasingly horizontal at higher numbers.

One way to determine whether an integer x is composite or not is to test whether it is evenly divisible by any integer i greater than 1 and less than the square root of x ($\sqrt{x}$). It is not necessary to test for larger i since those are the companion divisors of the ones less than $\sqrt{x}$. Remember that all divisors come in conjugate pairs ($i_1 < \sqrt{x}$, and $i_2 > \sqrt{x}$) except for the roots of perfect squares, in which case $i = \sqrt{x}$. This dual property of divisors is expressed in the symmetry of the square root boundary, which is the curve $y = \sqrt{x}$.

The image below illustrates this idea: in order to check if a number is composite or prime, you only need to refer to the shaded area at the top.

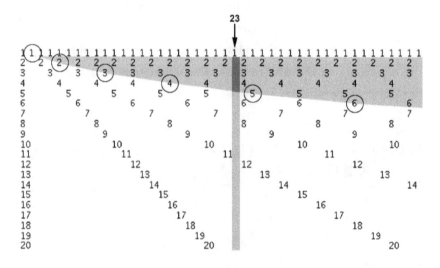

Notice that the number 23 has no divisors less than its square root (other than 1, which we don't count), and this is all that has to be checked to determine that it is prime.

Wolfram describes a kind of quadratic sieve that can generate the prime numbers, using the integer points lying on the parabola $x = y^2$. The image on the next page shows the sieve. It was lifted from a paper by Abigail Kirk, who refers to it as a "visual sieve", because it lets the primes be picked out visually. Kirk references Yuri

Matiyasevich and Boris Stechkin as the originators [4]. To build the sieve, plot a parabola on a grid as shown below in image (a). On each arm of the parabola, plot all the points (i^2, i) with i being a whole number, starting from 2, and stopping at some maximum value. Label the number using i. Then connect each pair of points occurring above and below the x-axis, as shown. The points where these lines intersect the x-axis correspond to composite numbers. Points where no lines cross are prime numbers.

The first thing I noticed when I saw this graph was that if you overlay the bottom half of this graph onto the divisor plot, the bottom arm of the parabola happens to lie on the square root boundary, as shown in (b).

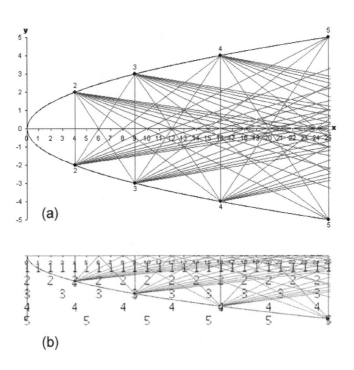

(a)

(b)

Not surprisingly, there is a lot of crossing of lines going on at divisor locations. Perhaps there is more to be learned from studying this overlay.

Symmetry

The illustration below shows D36. Its divisor pairs are (1, 36) (2, 18) (3, 12) (4, 9). And it has a perfect square root: 6. Notice that the two numbers in each pair in this series converge towards the square root boundary.

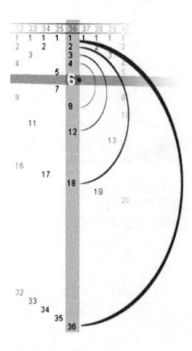

This is just a hint of the kind of symmetry that becomes more complex at larger numbers. For instance, the image on the next page shows the square root boundary at one million, with its square root 1000, indicated by the arrow.

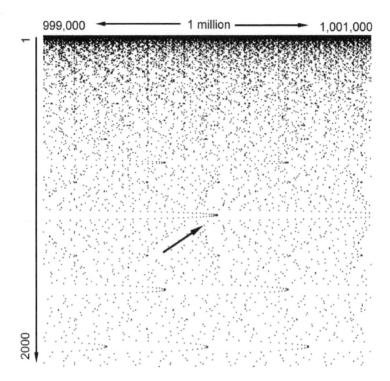

You may notice a parabolic shape with its vertex located at the square root of a million. What's up with that? The next chapter is all about these peculiar shapes: the *square root parabolas* of the divisor plot

4. Fantabulous Parabolas

Parabolas appear often in the physical world, and also in mathematical visualizations, such as what we have just seen in the previous chapter. Parabolas appear when you plot a graph of the

subdivision of sine waves into integer-number frequencies, like the harmonics in a guitar string, vibrating in halves, thirds, quarters, fifths, and so-on.

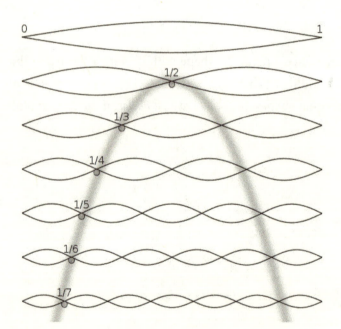

 A big surprise came when I started building the divisor plot on a computer, and could see the divisors of larger numbers. Looking closely at the square root boundary, I started to make out a series of parabolas, by connecting nearby dots. These parabolas are kind of like the cross-sections of compressed, folded pieces of lettuce in a Dagwood sandwich... or the curved edges of a folded blanket. Parabolas in the divisor plot represent a special view into the world of composite numbers. All parabola vertices point from left to right (from smaller numbers to larger numbers).

Upon first discovering these parabolas, one gets the intuitive sense that something interesting might be going at in these locations. It is almost as if an infinite series of fingers along the square root boundary are saying, "look here, look here!"

So let's look at these "square root parabolas". They are infinitely nested, and their vertices run along the square root boundary. On the next page is an example of the square root parabola located at x=100, and y=10 (the square root of 100).

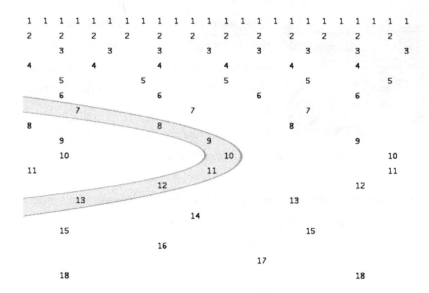

I will refer to the entire set of square root parabolas as *P*, and I will refer to individual parabolas with the value n, an integer that can range from 1 to infinity. Here is an equation that I came up with to describe the curve of any square root parabola *Pn*:

$$x = (n/2)^2 - (y - n/2)^2$$

In this equation, *y* ranges from 0 to n. Consider this as an exponential Diophantine equation (an algebraic curve that uses only integers). It defines a set of lattice points that correspond to sets of divisors, numbered 1 to n, as shown below. It appears as if the entire set *P fully tessellates* the divisor plot: it intersects every divisor. Every divisor pair is a member of one and only one square root parabola. This is illustrated in the image on the next page showing *P*1 through *P*8, indicated with straight lines connecting the ordinal series of divisors that lie on them.

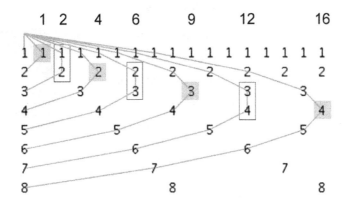

The arms of each parabola Pn stretch out to the left, intersecting the zero divisor drip at (0,0) and (0, n). Notice how each even-numbered Pn has a perfect square root divisor located at its vertex. Each odd-numbered Pn, on the other hand, does not have a single divisor but instead has a pair of divisors slightly to the left of where the vertex would lie. These two divisors have a difference of 1. That means their product is a *pronic number*: a number that has two divisors with a difference of one. Thus, the first three pronics, (2, 6, and 12), are represented here (not including 0, which can be expressed as 0 x 1).

All Pn have the same overall parabola shape. But due to their x locations on the lattice, even and odd-numbered Pn exhibit different spacing in x between their divisors, as shown here.

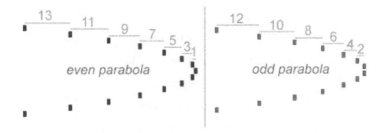

even parabola   odd parabola

An Observation about Square Numbers

Fibonacci observed that square numbers can be constructed as sums of consecutive odd numbers. Look again at the even-numbered parabola I just showed you. The x-spacing between divisor pairs corresponds to the series of odd numbers, counting from right to left.

Suppose that the vertex of this parabola were located at (100, 10). If you work leftwards from the vertex, and add the odd numbers shown, you get a series of squares: 1, 4, 9, 16, 25, 36, etc. Now, subtract each of these square numbers from 100. Subtract 1 from 100, and you get 99, which is the x value for the pair immediately to the left of the vertex. Subtract 4, and you get 96, which is the x value for the pair immediately to the left of that. Subtract 9 and you get 91... And so-on. Subtracting each of these square numbers from the x value of the vertex results in the x values for each pair of divisors on the parabola. Since we know that P represents a set of composite numbers, we arrive at the following general conclusion:

> *Take any square number x, and then take each square number less than x and subtract it from x. All the numbers in this set (except the lowest) are composite.*

Constant Sums

Rob Sacks (whose *number spiral* we will visit soon [9]) observed that all divisor pairs in a square root parabola Pn have the same sum. This was a creative leap: instead of focusing on multiplication, what about addition? Not only did he observe that the divisors have the same sum, but in fact the sums are all equal to the parabola's index, n. This leads to one definition of a square root parabola: "a square root parabola Pn

is the curve which intersects all divisor pairs in the divisor plot whose sums equal n."

I tested to see if any other divisor pairs besides those on the parabola have the same sum, and it appears that there are none. And so, my hypothesis is that a square root parabola contains *the only* divisor pairs with this constant sum. Therefore, a square root parabola Pn can be defined more simply as: "the set of conjugate divisors in the divisor plot whose sum is n". One test I did is illustrated below, with parabola $P48$, whose vertex is located at (576, 24). The illustration highlights numerals for the divisor pairs whose sums equal 96 (which is 48 x 2). The image is greatly stretched vertically to make it easier to see.

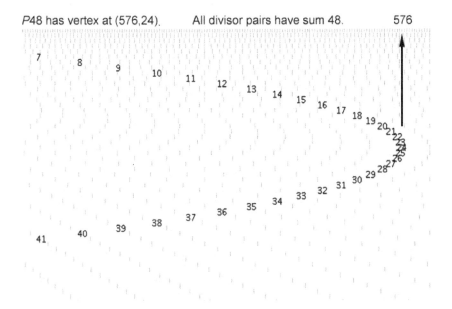

P48 has vertex at (576,24).   All divisor pairs have sum 48.   576

Properties of Divisor Pairs on Square Root Parabolas

The illustration on the next page shows divisors near the vertex of *P128*, located at (4096, 64). Notice how divisor pairs to the left of the vertex converge towards the square root boundary as they get closer, and that there are no divisor pairs immediately to the right. We will confront this mystery later on.

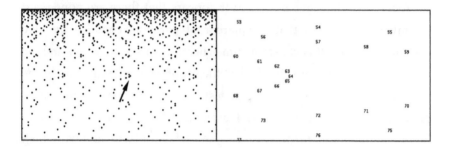

The illustration below shows *P2* through *P8*. Below them are symbols representing the products of the divisor pairs on these parabolas.

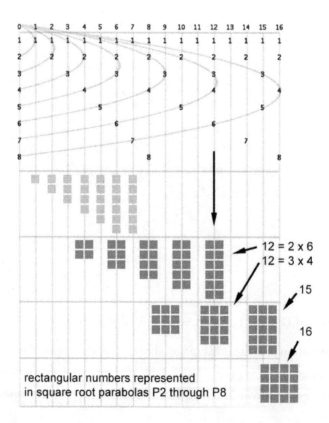

rectangular numbers represented
in square root parabolas P2 through P8

Each symbol in this illustration is a rectangular array of blocks, where the number of blocks is equal to the product. These symbols illustrate the idea of a rectangular number. The number of columns in the array equals the divisor on the top arm of the parabola, and the number of rows equals the divisor on the bottom arm of the parabola. The number of columns and rows is equal in the case of square numbers.

For example, the rectangular number 12 is shown as occurring on $P7$ and $P8$. The associated symbols show two of the three ways to express 12 (2x6 and 3x4). (The third way, 1x12, occurs on $P13$, which is not included in this illustration). This illustration may help give insight as to why these parabolas exist. The answer may have to do with the possible ways to arrange these blocks into rectangular arrays. Note that primes can only be represented in single-column, and that their divisors are always the second pair occurring at the left edge of a parabola (after the pair occurring at x=0).

Approaching *Squareness* at Infinity

As we observe the regions near the vertices of Pn at higher n, we see that their divisor pairs converge towards a ratio of 1. Since all Pn have the same shape, divisor pairs of numbers which are one-less than perfect squares converge towards "squareness", as n increases. For instance, compare the numbers 35 and 18,768, both of which are followed by a square number. Their closest divisors pairs are (5,7), and (136,138), respectively, as shown on the next page.

Even though each pair has a difference of 2, the ratios of those pairs are 0.714 and 0.985. Another way to express this is to refer to the rectangular arrays in the previous illustration. The rectangular arrays representing these pairs will appear more square in proportion at higher n.

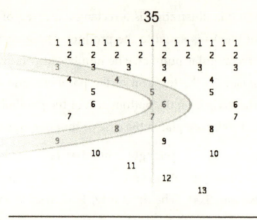

35

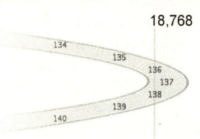

18,768

As an oak grows from a tiny sapling to a giant adult tree, the roots sink deeper into the soil and become longer. This is similar to what happens in the divisor plot. As n increases, the square root parabola series sinks lower and lower into the soil of divisors.

But trees have many many roots. And alas, so does the divisor plot: the square root boundary is not the only parabola-rich place in the divisor plot. As we delve deeper and rightward along the divisor plot, the roots accumulate in number and they sink deeper.

 Those "look here" fingers we saw earlier are pointing all over the place. In the next chapter, we will look at many varieties of parabolas, and try to get a better sense of why they exist.

5. Resonating Waves

Parabolas are scattered throughout the divisor plot, not just along the square root boundary. They are most clearly-visible among the divisors of the higher numbers. They come in many varieties, and I have reason to believe that each is nestled inside of a unique local environment.

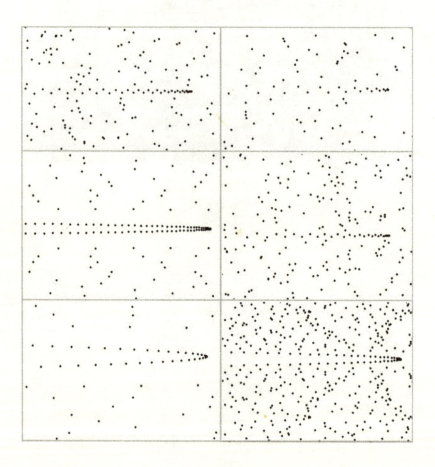

Long after discovering these parabolas, I came to realize that they can be interpreted as *resonating waves* among divisor pairs. In this chapter, we will come to an understanding of what makes parabolas resonate so much – not only in the visual mind, but in the relationships among their divisor pairs.

Let's start by looking at a special class of parabolas whose vertices lie at x which are powers of two ($x = 2^n$). The illustration below show a few such parabolas above and below the square root boundary in a window with the y range scaled 3 times the x range to make them easier to see. The square root boundary is indicated with a mostly-horizontal line. The left panel shows a pair of divisors located at the vertices of parabolas at $x = 8192 = 2^{13}$. The right panel shows a pair of divisors located at the vertices of parabolas at $x = 16384 = 2^{14}$, plus its square root.

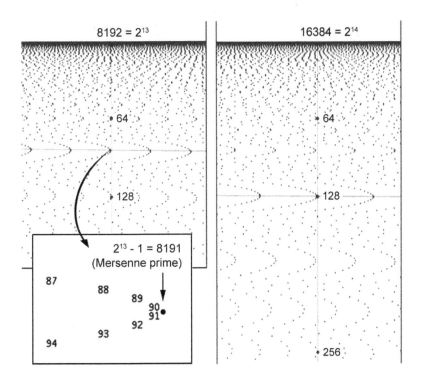

Mersenne primes are the primes of the form 2^n-1. There are gaps in x immediately to the left of these parabola vertices (such as the Mersenne prime $2^{13}-1$, indicated below). These visual gaps might help to provide some insight into the Mersenne primes.

Notice that the y values of these 2^n numbers are themselves 2^n numbers. It turns out that there are many curves in the divisor plot that contain 2^n parabolas, including the square root boundary itself (they are located at $x = 2^n$, where n is even, as we saw in the example of 2^{14}). Now take a look at this illustration:

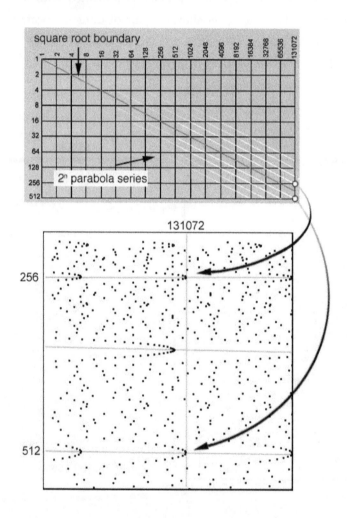

This image shows a schematic of these curves in the divisor plot. Both the x and y dimensions are scaled exponentially, so that $x = 2^n$, and $y = 2^k$. The values of n and k are integers, represented by the grid lines in the graph.

Notice that the square root boundary (the darker line cutting diagonally through the grid) appears straight as a result of this scaling. On either side of the square root boundary are white lines where 2^n parabola vertices lie (specifically, at the locations where the graph lines cross). Two examples of parabola vertices are indicated by dots at the bottom-right of the graph. Notice that the white lines start off transparent and get brighter towards the lower-right. I rendered them this way because it is difficult to detect 2^n parabolas at smaller x, or farther from the square root boundary. This is not to say that they don't exist - just that I was not able to identify any.

If you look closely in the image above you can make out a few parabola series that lie at y values sandwiched *in-between* the parabola curves represented in the graph. It appears that all parabola series follow similar curves.

In the image on the next page, we see a pair of parabolas lying above and below the square root boundary. Notice how each divisor is located on the opposite arm of the parabola in relation to the other divisor in the conjugate pair. These opposing arms contain conjugate divisors. This is a property of all the non-square root parabolas, which come in pairs. The illustration shows how the number 10366 is the product of 71 and 146, and it is also the product of 73 and

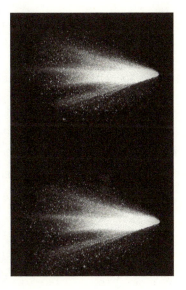

142. Is there any significance to the fact that these pairs are so close? Notice that 10368 has a pair of divisors each lying at parabola vertices.

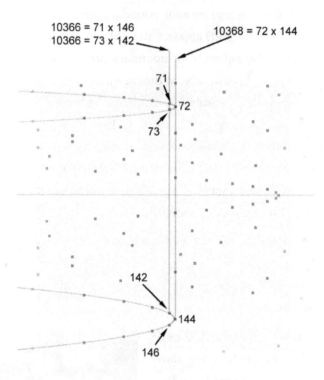

In order to better understand these parabolas, let us first explore the divisors that lie exactly on the vertices.

You may have noticed in the above example that 144 = 72 x 2. On the next page we see another example of pairs if parabolas whose vertices have the same relationship, i.e., the y value of the lower vertex is twice that of the y value of the upper vertex.

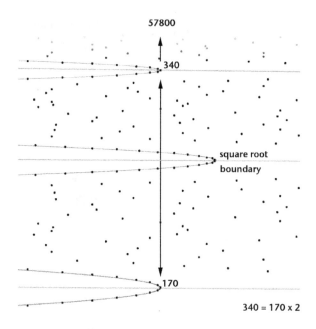

57800

340

square root
boundary

170

340 = 170 x 2

In the following image we see pairs of parabolas whose vertices have a different of one forth, i.e., 90 x 4 = 360.

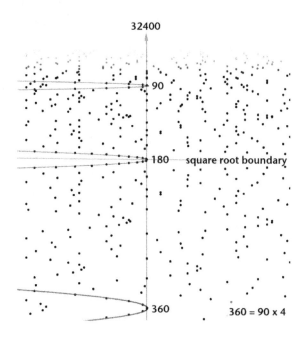

32400

90

180   square root boundary

360   360 = 90 x 4

49

We are finding parabola vertices with divisor pairs related by integer values. The illustration below shows a parabola at left, lying on the square root boundary with vertex at (4761, 69). It is represented by a square. At right is a pair of parabolas whose vertices are (4802, 49), and (4802, 98), This pair is represented by a 1x2 rectangle.

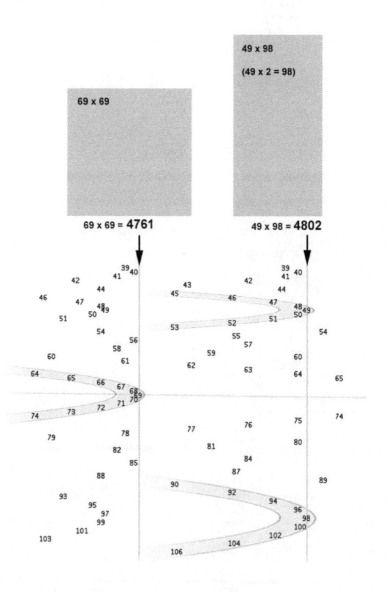

Below is an illustration of a larger area showing several streams of parabolas, in the vicinity of one million. This graph has been compressed in the horizontal axis to make the parabolas easier to see. Near the middle of the graph is shown the square root of one million (1000). Just to the left of that is shown a pair of divisors (707 x 1414) for 999698. These have a ratio of 2. To the left of that is shown a pair of divisors (577 x 1731) for 998787. They have a ratio of 3. Another pair of divisors is shown (500 x 2000) for one million. These have a ratio of 4. This graph shows parabola vertices corresponding to divisor pairs with integer-number ratios.

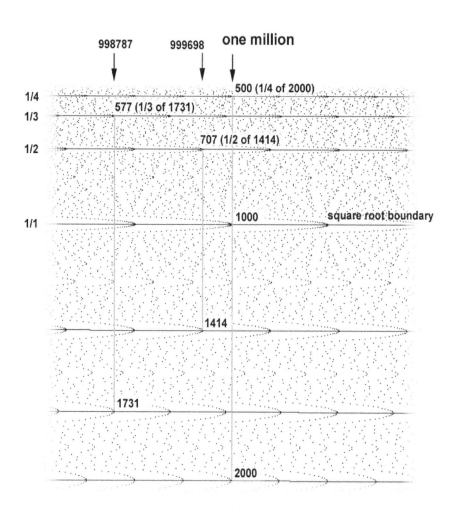

With this discovery that parabola vertices are associated with divisor pairs with integer ratios, I found that I could plot a subset of divisors to view parabolas more clearly. The illustration below shows the region near the square root of one million, with only certain divisors visible, according to a threshold criterion: only divisors that come in pairs whose ratios are close to an integer value, using an arbitrary cutoff threshold chosen to maximize parabola visibility.

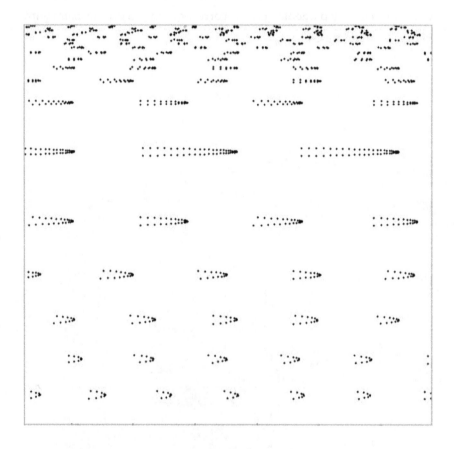

Presto! We now know how to isolate parabolas in the divisor plot using math, and not just our eyes.

In fact, given this knowledge, it's very easy to predict where a parabola vertex is living in the divisor plot without ever having to lay your eyes upon it. All you have to do is pick a number (say, 347), and then multiply it by some integer (small ones are easiest – say, 3). In this case you end up with 1041. Now, multiply 347 by 1041, and you get 361227. Your mystery parabola lives at x=361227, y=347. You can confirm this by visiting 361227 on the number line, and then scrolling down along the divisors until you get to your original number: 347. There you will see a lovely parabola vertex, waiting for your visit, smiling sideways at you.

Parabolas and Exponentiation

Considering the discovery of the square root parabolas and the 2^n parabolas, I wondered if there might be some connection between exponentiation and the existence of parabolas. The illustration below makes this question visual – it shows the three usual operations of ordinal numbers: addition, multiplication, and exponentiation.

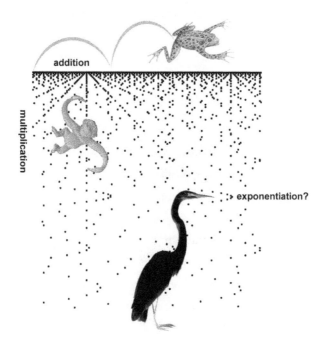

I am not sure if parabolas are associated with exponentiation in general, although there is at least a strong correlation to *squared* numbers.

Since we know that parabola vertices are associated with divisor pairs that have integer ratios, we can come up with the following bit of math:

Product x is equal to y1 times y2. If y2 is twice the size of y1, we can express x as:

$$y1 \times y1 \times 2 \qquad or \qquad y1^2 \times 2$$

If y2 is five times the size of y1, then it can be expressed as:

$$y1 \times y1 \times 5 \qquad or \qquad y1^2 \times 5$$

In both cases, we end up with one squared value and a multiplier. We can generalize this to:

$$y1 \times y1 \times n \qquad or \qquad y1^2 \times n$$

This is consistent with a discovery that Rob Sacks made while exploring parabola series. He observed that every parabola below the square root boundary can be generated by taking a square root boundary parabola and scaling all its 2D divisor locations by an integer n. Its complimentary parabola (lying above the square root boundary) can be found by dividing the y values of those divisors by n. This is illustrated on the next page. The square root parabola P6 at left has both the x,y values of all its divisors multiplied by **n = 2** to create the larger, fatter parabola at lower-right. Dividing the y values of those divisors by **n** generates the smaller, skinnier parabola above that.

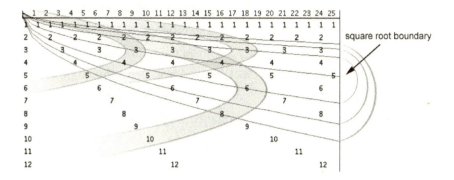

All derived parabolas fall along curves above and below the square root boundary, as shown below. This scaling in y may explain why parabolas are fatter below the boundary and skinnier above the boundary. Each of these curves can be expressed as follows:

$$y = (\sqrt{x}) \times n$$

And so, the curves that complimentary parabolas lie on can be expressed as:

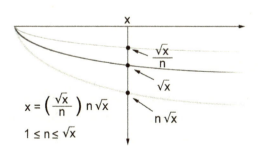

Resonance

I have started to think of parabolas as representing the places in the divisor plot where divisor pairs resonate with each other by whole number values. The strongest resonating wave is at the square root, where divisor pairs are close to the same (or identical in the case of the roots of perfect squares). Slightly less resonating are the divisor pairs that have a relationship near 2 to 1, as we have seen. And slightly less than that are the ones with a relationship near 3 to 1. And so-on. Perhaps thinking in terms of resonance might help us get a better understanding as to why these parabolas exist.

Why Do Parabolas Point In One Direction?

There is a fundamental question that David Cox raises: why are the arms of these parabolas all left-opening? [2] (I like to describe the parabolas as waves pushing rightward, but it doesn't matter – the question still remains: why is it not the other way around?) Cox points out that it remains to be proven that all parabolas are left-opening, and *why*. My suspicion is that all of them are indeed left-opening, and the reason is related to the way some divisor pairs converge towards integer ratios as you move along the number line towards larger numbers. For me, it is more productive to let my mind wander from left to right, in the direction of the pointing fingers – towards the higher numbers. The following imaginary scenario illustrates this direction of thought.

Sugar Cube Packaging

Imagine that you have 100 sugar cubes, and imagine that each sugar cube is 1x1x1 centimeters to a side. In order for them to fit snugly into a square tray, you need the tray to be 10 centimeters to a side. But if all you have is a 9 x 11 centimeter tray, you could put 99 sugar cubes in the tray, although you have to toss out one sugar cube. It's not a square, but pretty close, as shown at left in the following illustration.

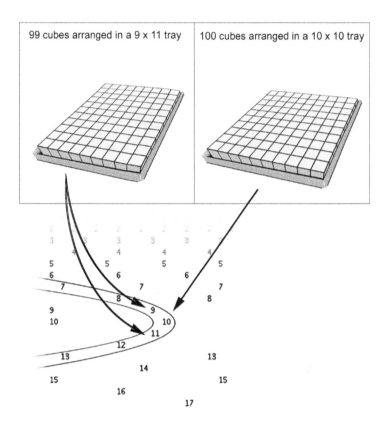

In this illustration these sugar cube trays are associated with the two highest x values of parabola P20. Again we encounter the notion of *squareness* and *almost squareness*. The 9 x 11 tray of 99 sugar cubes is as close as you can get to a square tray of 100 cubes without going over 100. If you prefer square trays, it's the next best thing. Your other choice is to get an 11x11 tray, but then you would have empty space in the tray without any sugar cubes.

The illustration on the next page shows what various sugar cube trays would look like if viewed from the top, corresponding to divisors along P20. Look at the path that traverses the curve of the parabola, crossing over the square root of 100: its divisor pairs flip over and trade places at that point. This path is represented in the schematic graph at the right of the illustration.

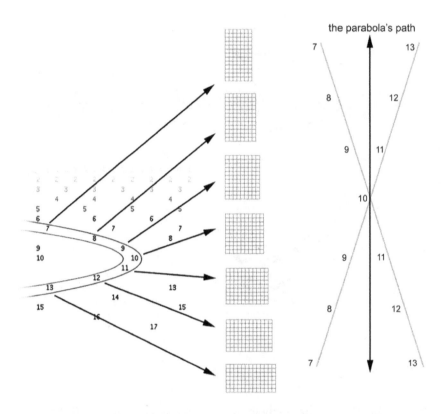

the parabola's path

Contrast the parabola's nonlinear path with the linear path of the number line, which marches from left to right. As the number line approaches 100, the divisor pairs near the square root boundary converge on the parabola's vertex. And then, suddenly: POOF. No more divisors! We have landed on the number 101 (which happens to be a prime). My question is: why do we not find any numbers that have divisors close to the square root boundary…until we get to 104? What accounts for this "squareless" gap?

First Day at the Factory

A little narrative might help enhance intuition. Imagine that you work at a sugar cube factory, and your job is to put the cubes into large, flat, square trays, and package them for shipping. It's your first day on the job. You have been instructed to package as many sugar cubes into a single square tray as you can. You see that there are many square (and almost square) trays, and there are many different sizes. So, you start by grabbing the biggest tray you can find, and you begin filling it with sugar cubes.

The first tray you grab happens to be a 9x9 tray. You start filling it with sugar cubes, packing them tightly. Soon it gets filled up, and you look around to see if there are any bigger trays. You find one that is slightly bigger (9x10, to be exact), and then you move all the cubes into that tray, and you continue adding more cubes. Soon, that tray gets filled up, and you decide to find a bigger tray (10x10). You soon discover that this factory is well-stocked with large square trays, and if you are willing to look around, you'll find a bigger tray to put the cubes in. This process is illustrated below.

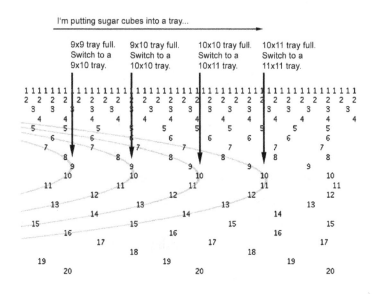

This little narrative has a rhythm: For each cycle, something changes gradually (adding more cubes), and then there is a sudden change (switching to a new tray). This rhythm is echoed in the illustration of the vertices of the square root parabolas P18 through P21. As you scan from left to right along a parabola, its width tapers down until it reaches its vertex and then...poof...empty space (like the new space in the bigger tray which will get filled up with more sugar cubes). Then the cycle repeats itself.

What I have just described to you is a qualitative description of both the directional and rhythmic character of the square root parabolas, rather than a mathematical explanation for why these parabolas point in the direction that they do. So, we are still left without a satisfactory answer. I'm not even sure if I have *qualitatively* answered the question as to why *almost identical* (or almost integer-ratio) divisor pairs sit *to the left* of parabola vertices, and not *to the right*. I feel as if we are close to arriving at a conjecture, but we are not there yet! Hopefully my qualitative description will provide some narrative lubrication for those of you with good math brains.

Listen to the Resonating Waves

Parabolas in the divisor plot are both aesthetically compelling as well as mathematically rich. Their existence raises many questions. For instance, could it be that ALL parabola series tessellate the entire domain of the divisor plot, as we have noted with square root parabolas? If so, perhaps composite numbers might be described in terms of all the parabola series that contain their divisors.

Now that we have explored the parabolas, let us now move onto another interesting aspect of the divisor plot. I have mentioned Rob Sacks a few times. He discovered a nice way to view numbers, and his explorations are very compatible with the divisor plot.

6. Relation to the Number Spiral

The Ulam Spiral is a graph of the prime numbers arranged in a rectangular spiral. Diagonal patterns can be seen throughout the spiral [10].

```
37-36-35-34-33-32-31
 |                 |
38  17-16-15-14-13  30
 |   |           |   |
39  18  5 — 4 — 3  12  29
 |   |   |       |   |   |
40  19  6   1 — 2  11  28
 |   |   |       |   |   |
41  20  7 — 8 — 9 — 10  27
 |   |               |
42  21-22-23-24-25-26
 |
43-44-45-46-47-48-49...
```

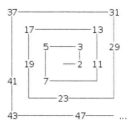

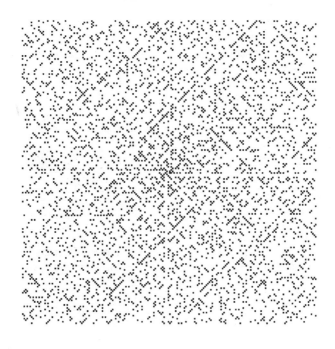

Robert Sacks discovered another way to arrange the primes: in a circular spiral. Below at left is an illustration showing the construction of the number spiral [9]. I lifted it from Sacks' web site (www.numberspiral.com). The number spiral is described as follows: roll the number line like a ribbon counterclockwise such that the perfect squares (0, 1, 4, 9, 16...) line up at right. This is shown in the illustration below at the upper-left. To the right of that is shown the first 2026 numbers as dots. The bottom of the illustration shows the patterns among the first 2026 primes, and the first 46656 primes in the number spiral.

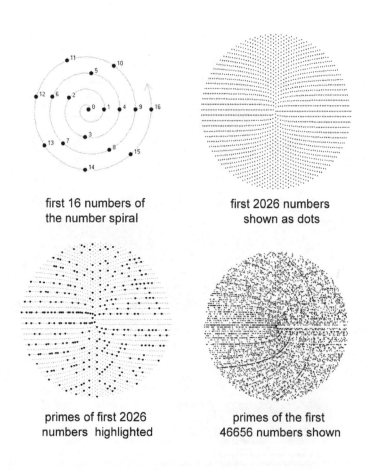

first 16 numbers of
the number spiral

first 2026 numbers
shown as dots

primes of first 2026
numbers highlighted

primes of the first
46656 numbers shown

I decided to try the *inverse* of showing the primes, and instead to show composite numbers, plotted here with gray values determined by the divisor function d(x) for all numbers x in the spiral. In this illustration, white indicates d(x) = 2 (primes), and black indicates d(x) = 20 or

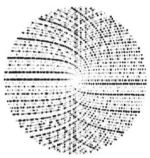

more. This is another way to visualize the idea that primes are just holes in overlapping composite number patterns

Product Curves

In his web site, Sacks shows several remarkable properties of number spirals. For instance, he describes a series of continuous functions that can be mapped as curves onto the spiral. The first curve, shown in the illustration below labeled "S" contains the perfect squares.

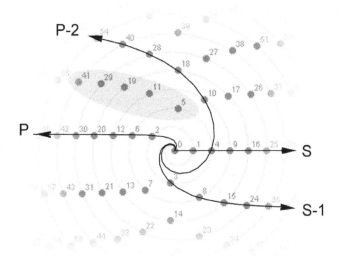

It is the only straight curve. The second curve, labeled, "P", shoots off to the left, in the opposite direction as the S curve. It traverses the

pronics (products of divisors with a difference of 1). The curve which contains numbers that are the products of divisors with a difference of 2 is shown just below the S curve. It is called the "S-1 curve". The curve which contains numbers which are the products of divisors with a difference of 3 is called the "P-2" curve.

Notice the cluster of primes (5, 11, 19, 29, and 41) lying on a curve in-between the P and P-2 curves. This is just one of the many prime-rich curves that extend outward (and tending leftward) in the number spiral.

Now let's take a look at how these curves relate to the divisor plot. The S curve corresponds to the square root boundary and it traverses the vertices of the square root parabolas. In the illustration below, the S curve has one of its perfect squares (5 = √25) highlighted with a circle. Notice that the divisor plot has pairs of curves corresponding to all of the curves in the number spiral. The S curve is the only one that does not map to a double-curve in the divisor plot. Four examples of x   (24, 25, 28, and 30) have their divisor pairs indicated with circles - this is meant to emphasize the fact that all of Sacks' product curves refer to divisor pairs.

And here is something interesting about the cluster of primes we just saw on the number spiral: each one of those prime numbers is followed by a pronic number, and in the illustration below there is a corresponding gap immediately to the left of the pronics in the divisor plot.

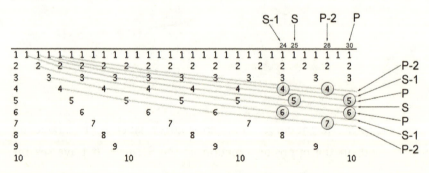

We could continue mapping the product curves from the number spiral onto the divisor plot as shown - forever. It appears that every divisor pair would be visited by a pair of product curves. Now it's time for a new way to classify divisors: let's refer to a pair of product curves on the divisor plot as Cn, where n of 0 corresponds to the square root boundary, and where increasingly higher values of n correspond to pairs of product curves that are increasingly farther away from the square root boundary. An algorithm for specifying Cn (provided by Sacks) is as follows:

```
y1 = (n+2*i)/2 - n/2
y2 = (n+2*i)/2 + n/2
x  = y1 * y2;
```

....where n is the difference between divisors, and, for each n, i is an integer that varies from 0 to infinity.

Another way to describe these curves is with the following equation (also provided by Sacks)...

$$y = \sqrt{x + \left(\frac{n}{2}\right)^2} \pm \frac{n}{2}$$

Notice in the image above that the divisors lying on each product curve increase by 1 as the curve extends to the right. They comprise an ordinal set of integers. We have seen a similar property with two other structures: zero reflection rays, and square root parabolas. Now we have a third way to organize divisors as sets of ordinal integers in the divisor plot. We will look at all of these ordinal curves in the next section.

Rolling the Divisor Plot onto the Number Spiral

The relationships between the number spiral and the divisor plot are numerous. And in fact, Rob Sacks had done preliminary explorations similar to mine before working on the number spiral.

Just as the number spiral takes the 1-dimensional number line and coils it up to occupy a disk, the divisor plot (a 2D graph) likewise can be rolled up like a scroll to occupy a cylindrical volume, corresponding to the number spiral, as illustrated below. Notice in the illustration below that the divisor plot is inverted so that the dense area is in contact with the number spiral.

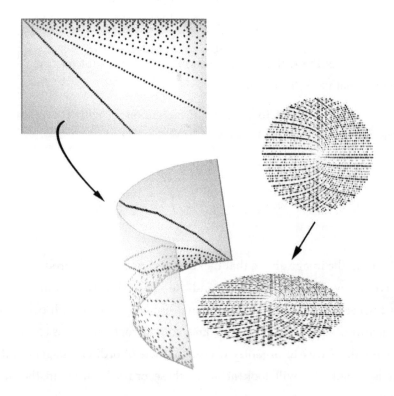

Now let's look at the rolled-up divisor plot in 3D. The image on the next page shows this volume rolled into a number spiral with 20000

numbers. Consider this as a 3D extension of the image above of the divisor function on the 2D number spiral. Vertical density of divisors in the 3rd dimension maps to color density in the 2D image.

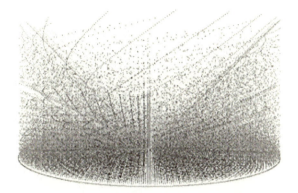

To help reduce clutter, I plotted only divisors less than the square root of x. However, it is still rather dense. So I decided to plot only conjugate pairs of divisors whose difference is less than or equal to 16. This is shown below. This illustration reveals the fact that the square root boundary, when rolled onto the number spiral, conforms to a cone. It also makes the S-curve and P-curve more clearly visible (they are lying at the left-most and right-most edges of the cone).

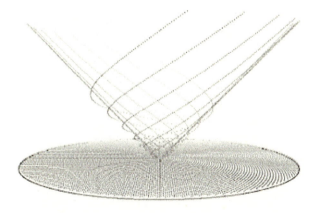

Notice the similarity to one of Sacks' illustration of some of the product curves:

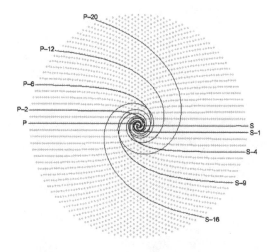

from Sacks: http://www.numberspiral.com

The next image shows only the divisors for the S-curve less than or equal to the square root of x. Notice the pattern in the triangle that looks like a piece of the divisor plot. But in fact, this pattern does not occur in the divisor plot. In the divisor plot, these Dx would be spread out and intermittent among many other Dx. The regularities in this pattern show some similarities among square numbers – interesting, eh? Something else to explore some day.

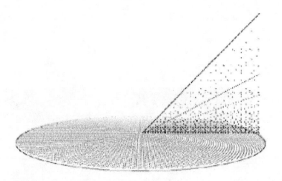

The next image shows the end of the square root parabola P200, whose vertex is at (10000, 100). It appears distorted because it is conforming to a curved surface.

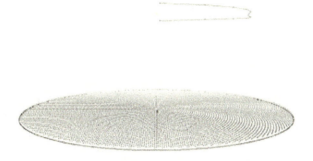

The number spiral is a canvas for visualizing regularities that occur along the number line, which are not easily noticed when viewed along a straight line. Like all things circular and spiral, the number spiral reveals periodic features - which the divisor plot is full of. There are likely more discoveries to be made by plotting divisors on the number spiral in new ways.

7. Many Divisors, Many Paths

columns (*D*)

rows (*R*)

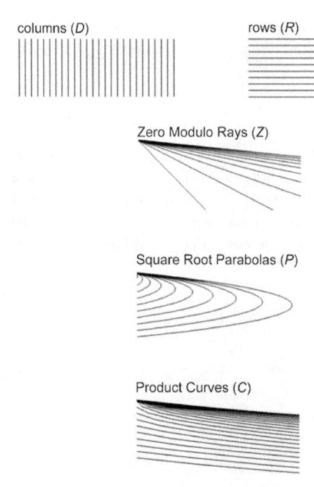

Zero Modulo Rays (*Z*)

Square Root Parabolas (*P*)

Product Curves (*C*)

I have identified five ways to classify divisors in the divisor plot.

1. Column Dx

When considered as a member of a column, a divisor is simply one element of the set Dx. This is the classification which began this whole exploration.

2. Row (Ry)

When considered as a member of a row Ry, a divisor is simply one of an infinite set of integers, which all have the same value - equal to its y coordinate. We have considered divisors along a row as representing a periodic signal over time, such as a blinking light or a beat in a musical polyrhythm. Differences in periods among rows are based on integers, and every possible integer period occurs in the set R. Seeing divisors as members of rows is one way to visualize the the Sieve or Eratosthenes.

3. Zero Reflection Ray (Zn)

When considered as a member of a zero reflection ray, a divisor is one of an infinite, ordinal set of integers ocurring along one of the zero reflection rays Zn.

4. Square Root Parabola (Pn)

When considered as a member of a square root parabola, a divisor is one of an ordinal set of integers from 0 to n, occurring on one of the square root parabolas Pn.

5. Product Curve (Cn)

When considered as a member of a product curve, a divisor is one of an infinite, ordinal set of integers, occurring on one of the product curves Cn.

The last three classifications are special: each consists of a set of curves, and each curve has an ordinal set of integers running through them. Let's take a good look at these last three classifications. Check out how each curve contains an ordinal set of integers.

Zero Reflection Rays (Z)

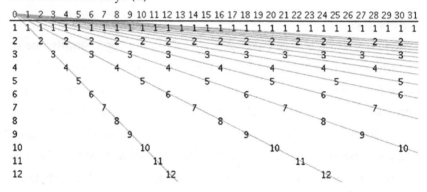

Square Root Parabolas (P)

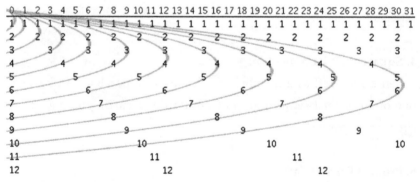

Product Curves (C)

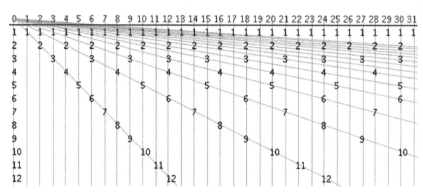

Below we see that divisors occur where Z intersects with D:

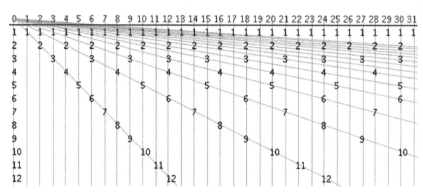

And here we see that divisors occur where P intersects with D:

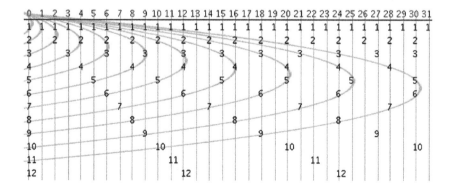

Divisors also occur where P intersects with Z:

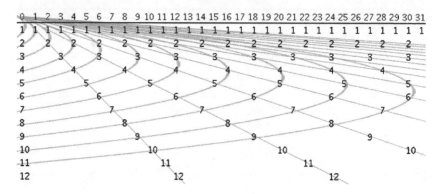

And where P intersects with C:

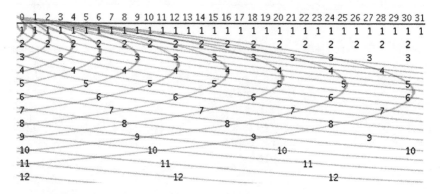

And where Z intersects with C:

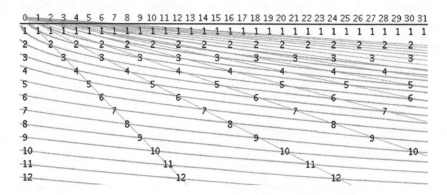

This implies that divisors occur at the intersections of P, C and Z:

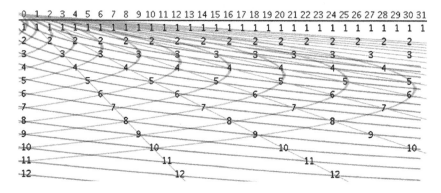

Finally, we see all of these classifications overlaid. Note that all 5 sets of curves (D, R, Z, P, and C) intersect at divisors locations.

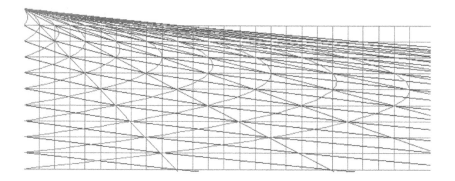

Given these classifications, we now have three ways to define Dx (besides in terms of divisors):

(1) Dx = the set of y values where x intersects P

(2) Dx = the set of y values where x intersects Z

(3) Dx = the set of y values where x intersects C

Observe that for any n, Zn and Rn are associated. The illustration on the next page shows that they each provide one of the divisors of a conjugate pair, whose product equals their x coordinate value. Two examples are illustrated: x = 14, and x = 24.

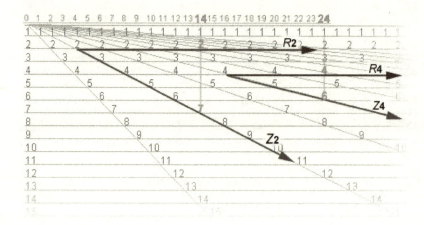

8. Emergent Patterns

Chaotic mixing can be illustrated by stirring paint, repeated folding, or some other iterative operation performed on a simple pattern, whereby it becomes increasingly complex. This kind of process can generate fractal images.

In chapter two we considered each row of divisors on the divisor plot as a periodic signal in time along x. The period of each row is equal to y. What happens if the periods are different? Would the same kinds of patterns emerge? The principle of sensitivity to initial conditions applies here: any slight difference in the period of some combination of these signals results in large differences over time (at large x).

To explore this, I made a variation of the divisor plot, ignoring any math and just considering pattern-formation from adjusting the periods. The image below shows this transformation.

There are eight panels: each showing a stage of the transformation. The top panel shows a rectangular array of dots. In the second panel, the rows of dots begin to expand rightward – but at differing rates: the top row doesn't expand at all and the bottom row expands the most. The difference in expansion among consecutive rows is linear. The last panel at the bottom shows the final result: the divisor plot.

Three distinct features emerge throughout this transformation: (1) diagonal linear features at the bottom-left (corresponding to the first few zero reflection rays), (2) small linear features at the top that come and go throughout the transformation (corresponding to divisor drips and reflection rays), and (3) a series of parabolas near the middle. The series corresponding to the square root boundary is the most distinct and robust throughout the transformation, becoming quite distinct by the third panel.

The robustness of this parabola series got me curious. So I made some variations on this transformation using non-linear shifts among the rows. These also produced parabola series that seemed equivalent (or at least analogous) to the square root boundary. Why are parabolas so common and robust? Answering this question purely from a pattern formation point of view might help to give us fresh eyes to look at the number-theoretical questions about parabolas.

Do Divisor Drips and Parabolas Avoid Each Other?

Parabolas and divisor drips (with their corresponding reflection rays) are perhaps the most visibly-striking features of the divisor plot. Is there some relation? We have already seen that there are many divisor drips – corresponding to spikes in the divisor function, where highly-composite numbers lie. I have a hypothesis: these two different features cannot be found near each other: in fact, they avoid each other! Think about this: divisor drips tend to be densest near the top of the divisor plot. Do any divisor drips reach down and traverse square root parabolas? After exploring parabolas in depth, we would not expect anything of the kind. Why, who would even think of interfering with the majestic flow of parabola waves pointing towards infinity!

But it may not be as simple as I have described it. Divisor drips have a clear origin (the top of the divisor plot, where density is 1), but their density tapers off as the drips fall downward. Where a divisor drip ends is perhaps just a matter of opinion. I leave it to you to either prove me right (there is something fundamentally incompatible about divisor drips and parabolas), or to prove me wrong (divisor drips and parabolas *can* live in harmony, and they have a secret collaboration that is not readily seen upon first glance).

The Divisor Plot is Self-Similar

When visualizing the structure of the number line, it is easy to find self-similar, scaling patterns, as Wolfram and others have shown, such as with the patterning in the binary expression of the number line – shown at right, in which 0 is light gray and 1 is black.

The family tree of composite numbers is self-similar. Every composite number is made of multiple copies of parts. Most composite numbers have parts made of parts made of parts, and so on. One way to appreciate the idea of fractal self-similarity is to create a fractal using pen and paper, and photocopy machine. Or else you could use a graphics application like Photoshop, with simple processes like cut-and-paste. The same works for the divisor plot.

You do not have to be a programmer to generate nice images of the divisor plot. Take a look at the illustration on the next page, which shows such a process. You will notice that at each stage, copies of copies of copies are made.

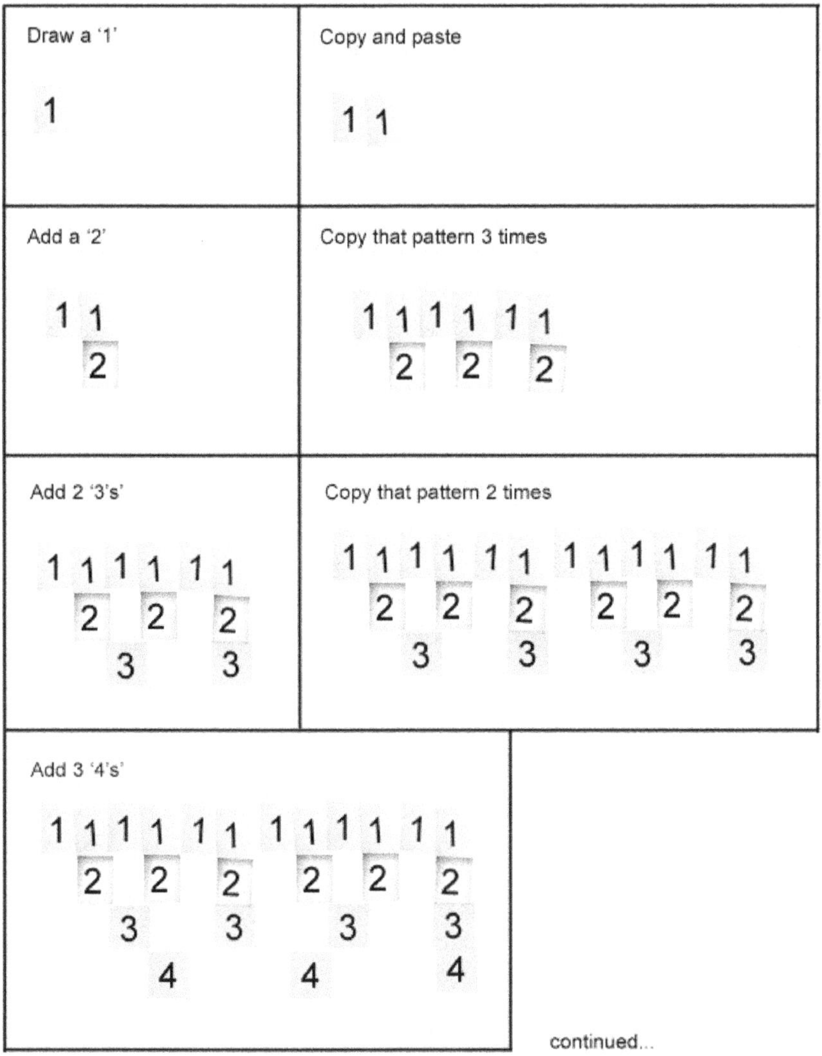

Draw a '1'	Copy and paste
1	1 1

Add a '2'	Copy that pattern 3 times
1 1 2	1 1 1 1 1 1 2 2 2

Add 2 '3's'	Copy that pattern 2 times
1 1 1 1 1 1 2 2 2 3 3	1 1 1 1 1 1 1 1 1 1 1 1 2 2 2 2 2 2 3 3 3 3

Add 3 '4's'

1 1 1 1 1 1 1 1 1 1 1 1
2 2 2 2 2 2
3 3 3 3
4 4 4

continued...

Each time a new row of numbers is added at the bottom, it is offset to the right by one unit, building the familiar diagonal zero reflection ray at the left. As you can see, the divisor plot is emerging before your very eyes.

You may have noticed something else in this accumulating pattern: the last column at the right of the pattern is always full of divisors, i.e., it is a solid divisor drip. Take a look at the next few steps:

Continuing on with this pattern:

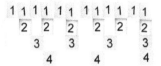

Copy that pattern 5 times

Add 12 '5's'

Add 10 '6's'

The zero reflection ray at the left of the pattern is increasing steadily, and a continuous divisor drip at the right is increasing as well. Nice and tidy! What a comfortable feeling to know that the left and right sides of this pattern provide orderly boundaries, keeping all that chaos inside.

Did you notice something else? The entire pattern is symmetrical. If you remove the divisor drip at the right, then you will find that the remaining left and right halves of the pattern become perfect mirror images of each other. We saw this earlier in the chapter on divisor drips while exploring the repetition of factorial patterns every n! number.

Something curious occurred while I was working out this construction algorithm: in order to insure a solid divisor drip at the right at each step, the exact number of numerals to add at the bottom, and the exact number of copies to make had to be precise. But, as the table on the next page shows, the series of parameters I chose is not orderly (or not apparently so). This is not what I expected at first. Check it out.

	quantity	numeral		num copies
Make	1	1	Copy the pattern	2 times
Add	1	2	Copy the pattern	3 times.
Add	2	3's	Copy the pattern	2 times.
Add	3	4's	Copy the pattern	5 times.
Add	12	5's		
Add	10	6's		

How do you explain the erratic series of numbers in the left and right columns? I will give you a hint: there should be another column of numbers in the table: at the very right I should have included a column of numbers listing the value of x, representing the number line, visualized as the length of the pattern at each step of the process.

Now, can you guess what the next step is in this process? I'll tell you the answer: "Copy that pattern 7 times." And there is another hint. It seems that the number of copies must always be a *prime number*!

Want to See More Structure? Visit a *Billion*...and Beyond
I would not recommend using Photoshop or a photocopy machine to construct the divisor plot as I have just demonstrated if you want to see the patterns in really large numbers. For that, you are advised to do a bit of programming, especially if you are interested in numbers whose names end in "illion".

Let's peer into the large numbers. On the next page is an image of a large area of the divisor plot at two billion. Notice that the parabolas appear flattened-out, and the spaces on either side of the parabola vertices are empty, as if they were bullets passing through a dusty cloud. Also, notice that there are many, many parabolas scattered throughout. Some of them seem to have appendages, puffs, and pseudopods extending out from them. Perhaps I am hallucinating. Perhaps I am exercising too much visual poetic license. On the other hand, this visual poetry is what motivates me (and I think you too :) to keep looking deeper.

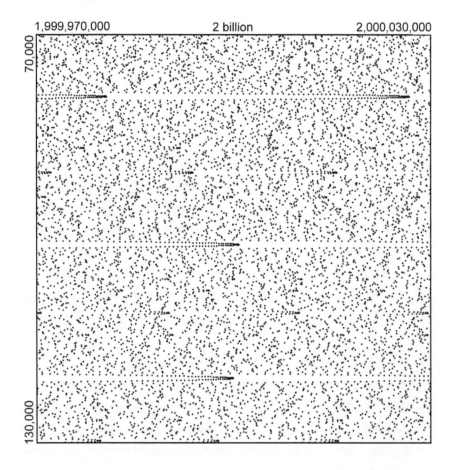

It seems that as we travel to higher numbers, these patterns exhibit more *kinds* of periodic structure. Perhaps the complexity is related to the hierarchical nature of large composite numbers – which are the products of smaller numbers, some of which themselves are the products of smaller numbers, and so-on – terminating in prime factorization.

Let's Visit One Quintillion: 1,000,000,000,000,000,000

One billion times one billion is one quintillion, or 10^{18}: one followed by eighteen zeros. Below is a view of the divisor plot ranging from one quintillion - 20,000 to one quintillion + 20,000, among the first 20,000 divisors. Not much to see here among such small divisors. In fact, the only thing this really shows is how the average density of the divisor plot ranges from 1 to 0, nonlinearly from top to bottom.

Let's scan downward and take a look at the square root boundary. Here we see the square root parabola whose vertex is located at y = one billion.

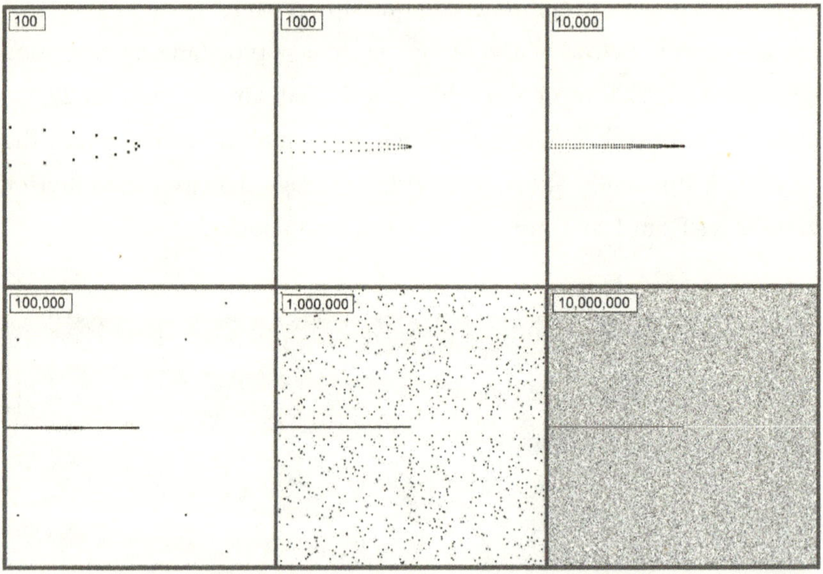

This illustration shows six consecutive magnifications outward, starting with a window of 100x100 and zooming out to a window of 10,000,000.

Notice how much empty space there is around this parabola's vertex, compared to the distance between consecutive divisors along the curve. At lower-left, we begin to detect a few divisors coming into view. As we zoom out farther, the square root parabola appears thinner, almost needle-like. This vast empty space around an otherwise dense parabola is something we have seen before. But it appears to become more pronounced in the higher numbers. What accounts for this property of the square root boundary? I invite you to come up with reasons (because I have no clue!)

Is one quintillion too small for you? Below is an image showing the square root of *nine* quintillion, in a 20,000,000 x 20,000,000 window.

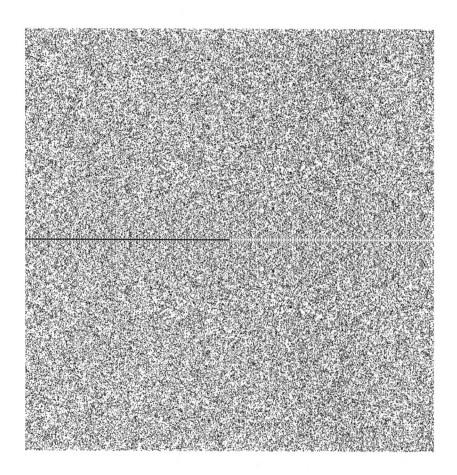

This image shows a lot of symmetry about the square root boundary. There may be some kinds of symmetry in other parts of this region, but we can't easily see it.

There is something else that is quite novel upon exploring these very large numbers. Let's set our gaze back to one quintillion now. If we scan down along the divisors to y = one million, we see a curious object, shown on the next page.

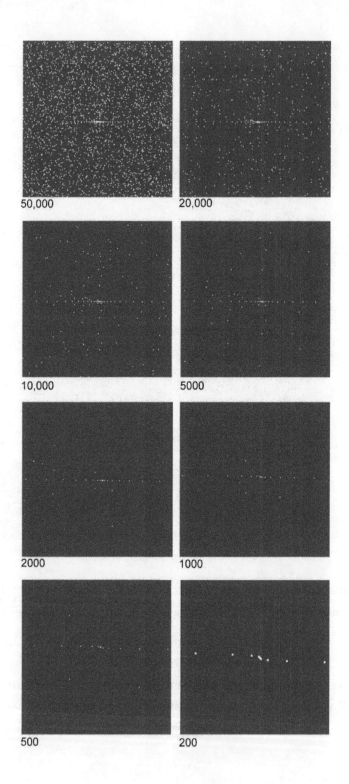

I have rendered the divisors in this object as white dots against black because it's fun to pretend like we are peering through a telescope at a distant galaxy. This series of images zooms in to this location, starting at a 50,000 x 50,000 window and ending at a window of 200 x 200.

Have we just discovered a new structure? Is this the result of numerical error in my code? This note of caution is based on the account of Benoit Mandelbrot's first sighting of the Mandelbrot Set, in which he thought there may have been error, causing the fractal-like artifacts, which turned out to be actual features of the Mandelbrot Set.

In the chapter on parabolas I described the phenomenon of parabola series occurring along curves defined by y = (√x) x n, and y = (√x) / n. These are the same as the product curves discovered by Rob Sacks. When x = one quintillion, then one million = (√x) / 1000. Based on this fact, I decided to explore other values of n. Below is an illustration showing features with n of 200 (left), 500 (middle), and 2000 (right), each in a window of 5000 x 5000.

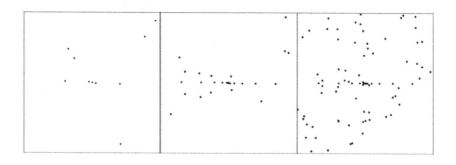

I then set x to 1024^3, which is 1,073,741,824, and looked at y = (√x) / n, with n of 32. A similar pattern is shown on the next page.

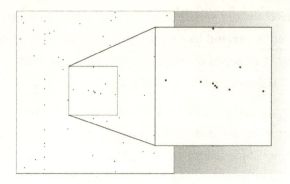

This little 3-divisor diagonal motif seems to pop up often, like a tiny descending flute melody. I discovered that this motif is always found at *cube roots*. I checked the small cube roots from 2 to 7, to make sure. The images below show the first few instances of this motif.

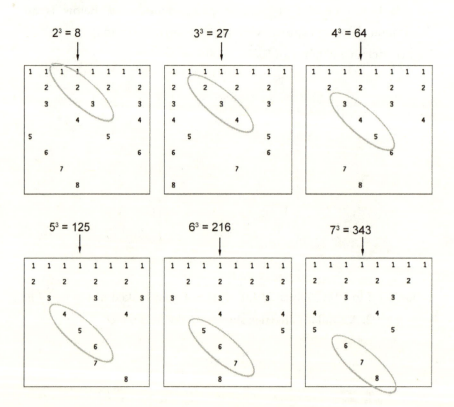

This motif continues on to the larger cubed numbers, as shown in the example below of 977 cubed. I then realized that the cube root of one quintillion is one million – I hadn't realized this earlier when we were looking at this divisor location. (In these examples, the y axis is scaled to make the numbers easier to read.)

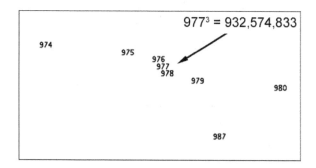

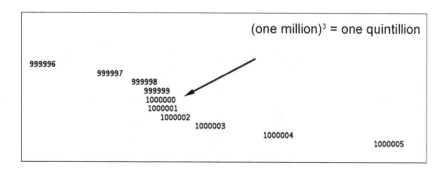

If all cube root divisors do indeed have this motif, then we have the following conjecture: all cube numbers greater than 2^3 have composite numbers as their immediate neighbors. No cube number has a prime neighbor.

One such cubed number I tested was $32^3 = 32768$. Its motif is shown on the next page. Notice that this motif is reflected about the divisor drip D32736.

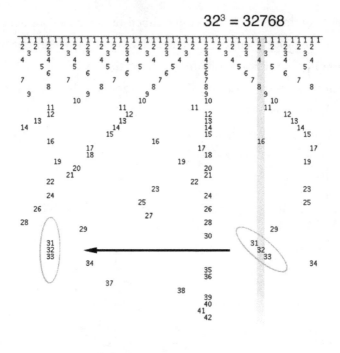

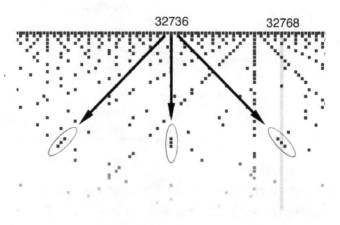

Beasts on the Horizon

I would not describe these flute motifs as "parabolas". But, might they be morphologically related? Distant cousins? My big question is this: do more novel structures like this lie at astronomically large regions of the number line? Do the *kinds* of structures continue to increase as well? Do these cube root motifs grow more appendages among the larger numbers? And what about other power numbers? Might those pseudopods we saw earlier be the embryos of something magnificent that awaits our eyes when we can explore numbers like 10^{1000}?

These motifs are perhaps the tip of a whole new iceberg waiting to be melted. Would you like to know the answers to these questions? Well, the reason I have no more answers is very simple: if I were to continue down this line of inquiry, and then address all the new questions that would result from consequent discoveries, I would NEVER FINISH THIS BOOK. The temptation to keep exploring, graphing, looking, writing, and conjecturing is enormous. And while the joy of discovery is a major motivation for this book, I need to stop at some point! (Happily, if you are reading this book now, I have somehow managed to finish it and get it into your hands).

We have accumulated many unanswered questions. And so, I would say that this journey has been a great success.

Randomness vs. Chaos

The digits in Pi are indistinguishable from a random sequence. If you search long and hard enough, you will find any sequence of digits in Pi, including your own phone number. Since the divisors in the number line are *not* random, I would *not* expect any possible pattern to be lying out there, no matter how far you look, such as the likeness of Elvis. But it does seem that there is more complexity and more kinds of complexity as I travel to higher numbers. So, I am very curious as to what may be found if I were to beef up my computer program to use gigantic numbers. This is certainly on my to-do list.

9. A New Appreciation of Number

Numbers are often described as having only one attribute: *size*. But in everyday experience, and in computer representations, unless they are very small (i.e., subitizable), numbers must be expressed as sequences of digits, or in algorithmic steps. In other words, they have structure. And the bigger they are, the more structure they have.

This structure becomes intricately hierarchical in the larger, highly composite numbers. The divisor plot is a portrait of the number line in expanded form, showing its beautiful structure – at least in terms of integer divisibility (there are other kinds of structure as well, such as partitioning).

This exploration may not provide immediate clues to prime number distribution. But it does reveal a variety of intriguing structures among the composite numbers, and so it may be used to enhance mathematical intuition - to let the visual brain be a lever for mathematical understanding. Like trying to see the forest but having difficulty because there are so many trees in the way, understanding the distribution of the primes might require shifting the focus to the composites. Composite numbers are metaphors for the structure of the universe. Seen in this light, the primes simply become a background to this beautiful, endless complexity.

A Personal Note

I am an artist, visual language evangelist, and computer programmer who enjoys discovering patterns. Of course mathematicians discover patterns as well. And so do economists, biologists, music theorists, historians, and psychologists. Maybe it doesn't really matter what we call ourselves.

I am not an advocate of learning math by rote methods. Traditional math is taught without emotion, aesthetics, discovery, analogy, or metaphor. Students are asked to learn rules and highly-abstracted equations and expressions, without knowing about the very human emotional and intellectual journeys that resulted in these distilled bits of language. Not only did I barely make it past Algebra in High School, but I failed the only Math course I ever took in college. Why? Here's one possible reason: it was taught by...a tape recorder! Each student had to work in a small cubicle with headphones, a tape recorder, and a rather gruesome workbook. There was no actual teacher - only a teaching assistant on hand to answer questions. There was always a long line of students waiting to talk to him. I believe that they were lined up because they yearned for interaction with a real human.

I agree with Lakoff and Nunez: Mathematics arises from the embodied mind [5]. Humans are a highly visual species. Our language is based on grounding metaphors. And math is the ultimate precise distillation of our language. While a mathematical gem can be a beautiful thing, it is meaningless without an understanding of how it came about – the story behind its discovery and its distillation. To ignore the experiential and exploratory aspects of math, and to only teach the rules and equations that are the end result of this deeply-human process – that is not good way to teach math to young people. That is an arrogant way to teach math.

To be perfectly honest, I am thankful that I failed mathematics in college, and that I feared and hated math for half of my life. Because when I decided to pursue computer programming as a way to explore visual language, I suddenly had a real reason to learn math. Having even the slightest amount of dyslexia can be a barrier to learning math using traditional approaches. But visual imagery can be used to stimulate the minds of nonlinear, visual, spatial-oriented thinkers, and to make math a joyful subject.

Following Buckminster Fuller's advice: "dare to be naïve", I set myself free to discover math in my own way, on my own terms, avoiding the narrow ruts and clichés, simply because I never learned them. With this fresh agenda, I choose to navigate clear of the cobwebs of history and academia. The ladder that I had constructed to climb out of ignorance is the same ladder that I use to climb ever higher, and grow more informed of traditional mathematics – now with a reason to care. As I develop from child-explorer to adult-child-explorer, I have found that a large community of like-minded people have also come out of the woodwork, thanks to the internet. They are communicating with me regularly on this subject. They range from young novices to (yes) professional mathematicians, and that is very exciting. We are all sharing in the joy of pattern-finding.

The computer is a programmable microscope for exploring the deep, dense fabric of numbers. That makes the mathematical experience much different than it was before computers were invented. Even more exciting: the internet is allowing people of many ages, races, cultures, and backgrounds to participate in the learning process, and to collaborate in the creation of new mathematical understanding.

Acknowledgments

I would like to thank Dr. David Burton, Professor of Art Education at Virginia Commonwealth University, where I failed Math. Dr. Burton encouraged me to pursue my love for patterns and geometry, which lead to an appreciation for math. Like Dr. Burton, I want to inspire young people to appreciate math through art and visual studies.

I also want to thank Robert Sacks, for making the number spiral, which influenced my approach, and after contacting him, for his many ideas and suggestions concerning relationships of the divisor plot to the number spiral - and for new discoveries in terms of parabolas.

Thanks to Ralph Abraham, mathematician and chaos theorist, for supporting my ideas and adding a link to the divisor plot in his web site: http://www.ralph-abraham.org/support/

Thanks to David Espinosa, for help with math, and for general brilliance. Thanks to Hector Sabelli for inspirational conversations, and a healthy viewpoint on how mathematics relates to art, psychology, and philosophy. Thanks to Tom Barbalet for great discussions on the nature of number and space, and for advice on the writing of this book.

And finally, thanks to Beth O'Sullivan, for her great mind, strong heart, wonderful homemade soup, and observations on prime number patterns.

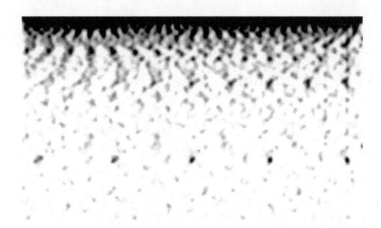

A region of the divisor plot, blurred to emphasize repetitive patterns.

References

[1]   Chaitin, G. Meta Math! The Quest for Omega. Pantheon. 2005 page 16

[2]   Cox, D. Visualizing The Sieve of Eratosthenes. Notices of the American Mathematical Society. volume 55, issue 5, page 579. 2008

[3]   du Sautoy, M. The Music of the Primes. Harper Collins, 2003. Page 34

[4]   Kirk, A. Catching Primes. +Plus Magazine, Issue 47, 2008. University of Cambridge Millennium Mathematics Project Centre for Mathematical Sciences Wilberforce Road Cambridge CB3 0WA. Website: http://plus.maths.org/content/catching-primes

[5]   Lakoff, G. and Nuñez. R. Where Mathematics Comes From: How the Embodied Mind Brings Mathematics into Being. Basic. 2000

[6]   Riemann, B. "On the Number of Primes Less than a Given Magnitude". In *Gesammelte Werke*, Teubner, Leipzig. 1859.

[7]   Rucker, R. Mind Tools – the Five Levels of Mathematical Reality. Houghton Mifflin Company, 1987.

[8]   Sabbagh, K. quoted in the book, What We Believe but Cannot Prove. Ed. Brockman, J. Harper Perennial, 2006. page 21

[9]   Sacks, R. Number Spiral. 2003. web site published online at: http://www.numberspiral.com/ © 2003 – 2007 by Robert Sacks

[10] Stein, M. L., S. M. Ulam, and M. B. Wells. 1964, A visual display of some properties of the distribution of primes. AMA 71(May):516-520.

[11] Thomasson, D., From Knight Moves to Primes. 2001. web site published at http://www.BordersChess.org/KTprimes.htm © 2001 by Dan Thomasson

[12] Tomes, R. Harmonics Theory - The Physics and Maths: web site address: http://ray.tomes.biz/maths.html

[13] Ventrella, J. Prime Numbers are the Holes Behind Complex Composite Patterns. Presented at the International Conference on Complex Systems 2007, October 28-November 2, Boston, MA. web site: http://knowledgetoday.org/wiki/index.php/ICCS07/240

[14] Wolfram, S. 2002. A New Kind of Science. Wolfram Media, Inc. page 132

About the Book

This is version 2.0 of the book. It is a work in progress. A lot of the math is still quite sketchy and wobbly. Like software running on the internet (and possibly many e-books of the future) it is intended to evolve interactively as readers give feedback and make contributions. I believe the future of the book is highly interactive and collaborative. And I would like this book to continually evolve – with your help. You are invited to contact me at Jeffrey@Ventrella.com with comments or suggestions.

About the Software

The divisor plot is available as an interactive Java applet, available online at www.divisorplot.com.

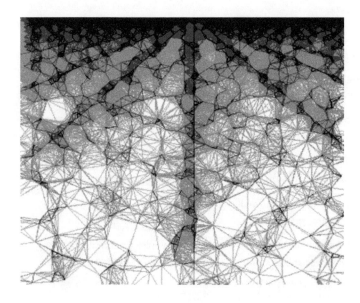

The number of pages in this book is 101.

$$101 = 10^2+1$$